JAK

CARTOONS No. 20

from

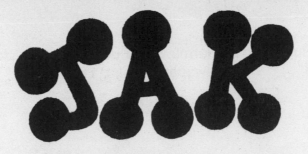
Evening Standard

and

The Mail ON SUNDAY

Published by Harmsworth Publications Ltd., for
Mail Newspapers p.l.c., London

ISBN 0 85144 498 9

Distributed by Seymour, Windsor House,
1270 London Road Norbury SW16 4DH (newstrade)
and Biblios, Partridge Green, Sussex RH13 8LD (booktrade)

Printed in Great Britain by
Spottiswoode Ballantyne Ltd., Colchester and London

September 9, 1987

For 38 pence a minute you could pass on sexy messages, all part of British Telecom's services.

"Hello! Luscious Linda here! I'm wearing a thick woolly vest and gum boots ... for further titillation put another 10p in!"

Wells Cathedral decided
to use poison to get rid of
troublesome pigeons ...

"We'd just got to 'All
things bright and
beautiful, all creatures
great and small' when
the biggest pigeon in
the world fell on him!"

September 17, 1987

Many people were said to be drawing dole illegally.

"Arthur! Isn't this the day you usually go to the dole office?"

September 18, 1987

On his first day at nursery school Prince Henry made a pair of binoculars out of two toilet roll tubes.

"I say! One can't find any toilet paper!"

September 20, 1987

Chief Constable James Anderton suggested that rapists should be castrated.

"I wish you'd stop telling everybody I've been 'dealt with' by the Chief Constable of Manchester!"

September 21, 1987

The Duchess of York, visiting America, became very upset at the sight of a snake.

"Anybody seen the Duchess of York?"

September 22, 1987

Fortune magazine issued a list of the world's richest people with the Queen ranking fifth (but the richest woman)

"That's funny, from what we've seen on TV, I would have thought Joan Collins had more money than you!"

Jeffrey Archer's play was not critically well received but was booked up for weeks ahead.

"Now if the critics will gather on platform three, Victoria Station, they will receive an envelope!"

September 25, 1987

The Government lost their appeal in Australia to stop former MI officer Peter Wright publishing his Spycatcher book.

"So far the legal fees come to approximately £10,000,000 - wouldn't it have been cheaper to have increased the old codger's pension in the first place?"

Sam Torrance, the golfer, announced his engagement to actress Suzanne Danielle although still married at the time.

"Not now, Suzanne, not now!"

September 29, 1987

For the first time, Europe won the Ryder Cup golf contest in America ...

"Is there any other business?"

BBC and ITV said they were going to play down the violence in TV programmes.

"We're remaking The Professionals without the violence!"

October 2, 1987

Mark Phillips, charged with driving at nearly 104 mph on the motorway, was fined £120 with costs and had his licence endorsed.

"Who do you think you are, driving at that speed, Mark Phillips' mother-in-law?"

October 9, 1987

Home Secretary Douglas Hurd announced plans to make it illegal to carry a knife without good reason and to ban such offensive weapons as knuckledusters ...

"I thought they looked nicer when they carried those knives!"

The fascination of the Loch Ness monster ... a sonar scan investigated the length of the loch to no avail.

"Have they gone yet?"

October 13, 1987

An army sergeant was accused of maltreating recruits …

"Better untie the Adjutant, Colonel, the Army brutality investigation team's turned up!"

October 15, 1987

Two more people were charged in connection with the Guinness takeover of Distillers

"That's the trouble with this country! - one law for the poor, and one law for the rich!"

October 16, 1987

Short take-off planes began flights to Paris from London's Docklands Airport.

"I thought it was a number eight to Bethnal Green!"

October 19, 1987

Hurricane force winds brought down thousands of trees in London and the South East.

"This could be our best day ever!"

October 20, 1987

Weathermen failed to forecast Southern England's hurricane ...

"His head covered by a blanket, yet another weather forecaster is taken in for questioning!"

BP share sale price was
announced by Marines
abseiling down a City
building - but the marke
fell dramatically.

"I wish you'd make up
your bloody minds!"

October 27, 1987

Shares were plummeting worldwide ...

"Jackson's beginning to show signs of stress!"

October 29, 1987

A report said that sex wa a good cure for headaches.

"You're quite right, Mr O'Reilly - my headache's completely gone!"

October 30, 1987

By closing day for buying BP shares, the market price was way below the fixed offer figure.

"What happens if they go up, Arthur?"

November 3, 1987

The Chinese hierarchy decided to clear out some of the older men.

"Hang on! That one's only eighty five!"

November 4, 1987

The Secret Service appointed an Ombudsman so that agents could have someone with whom to talk over their problems.

"What a ridiculous appointment! ... Why, Sir Philip's not even in the KGB!"

November 5, 1987

Some Coldstreamers were found guilty at a court martial and dismissed the service fo assaulting a recruit.

"Ah, lieutenant! Did you tell the men I won't tolerate bullying in this battalion?"

November 8, 1987

The Duke and Duchess of York were given planning permission to build their house on Green Belt land near Windsor Castle.

"The Duke of York's walls made no difference to us. Mind you, we haven't seen Granny since they bricked up the loo!"

Dessie O'Hare (known as the Border Fox) was twice caught by Irish Republic Police in connection with the kidnapping of a Dublin dentist and twice escape

"Well if it is the Border Fox - you arrest him and I'll catch him when he escapes"

It's planned to turn
Colditz Castle into a
luxury hotel.

"Your bill, mein Herr"

Richard Branson
introduced his Mates
brand of condoms.

"No! no! I really do
want a packet of
cotton wool."

November 15, 1987

The Church of England Synod debated the question of gay vicars and defeated a move to have them unfrocked ...

"I know we didn't want a gay vicar, but did we have to have such a blasted miserable one?"

November 16, 1987

If a vicar wanted to reassure his parishioners ...

"It's stopped all the malicious gossip about."

November 18, 1987

Ken Livingstone, MP, said that the IRA would eventually drive the British army out of Ireland.

"Let's hope your Ken Livingstone can do for the IRA what he did for the GLC!"

November 19, 1987

Michael Grade left the BBC to take over Channel 4 from Jeremy Isaacs.

"You do that once more Mr Checkland and Doris and I are off to Channel 4!"

November 22, 1987

A postal strike was threatened before Christmas.

"Look children, that's the man who won't be bringing your Christmas presents this year."

November 24, 1987

Student nurses were concerned that unlike other students they might have to pay poll tax - the Government said they would be entitled to a rebate.

"Seven of you gorging yourself on one sausage - well I'm the poll-tax inspector!"

November 26, 1987

The *Good Food Guide* said that some London restaurants had put up their prices way over the rate of inflation.

"Block all the exits men, we're ready to give table five the bill!"

Not everyone has to rely on the NHS ...

"For another fiver we could get rid of those spots altogether!"

November 30, 1987

The go-ahead was given to other companies to install telephone kiosks.

December 1, 1987

A poll of people who work there showed they did not like the new Lloyds building.

"I don't know about the interior design, I could never find my way in!"

December 2, 1987

Asians were found in secret compartments in a German van at Dover.

"Get ein shoehorn Otto, ve haf got ein double-booking!"

December 3, 1987

Prince Charles continue
to be frank about moder
architects.

"Oh! Charles, come
and see what the
architects have put in
the garden!"

December 6, 1987

Archbishop Runcie was frankly criticised in the anonymous preface to the new edition of Crockford's

"... then the Colonel said never mind Archbishop Runcie he didn't think much of the Vicar either. Well, one thing led to another ..."

December 8, 1987

The wife of a master at Millfield heard he was having an affair and attacked him during a lesson.

"Yesterday in science we learnt a lot of swear words and practised our first aid!"

December 10, 1987

A report said that many people died each year through mistakes by surgeons and anaesthetists.

"We had a run of bad luck, but I'm sure our anaesthetist has got it right this time!"

December 11, 1987

During the second Test a Faisalabad, England cricket skipper Mike Gatting and Pakistan umpire Shakoor Rama had a difference of opinion ...

"... And, now as a British task force starts its epic journey, we examine the origins of the dispute, starting with the first decision of the Pakistan umpire!"

December 14, 1987

It was reported that nurses had to take part-time jobs to make ends meet.

"Do stop moaning Doris, you won't eat better anywhere in the NHS!"

December 15, 1987

According to an interview in a women's magazine, the Manchester Chief Constable said he would like to flog criminals (he said afterwards he was misquoted).

"Oh, look! It's the Chief Constable's flogmobile!"

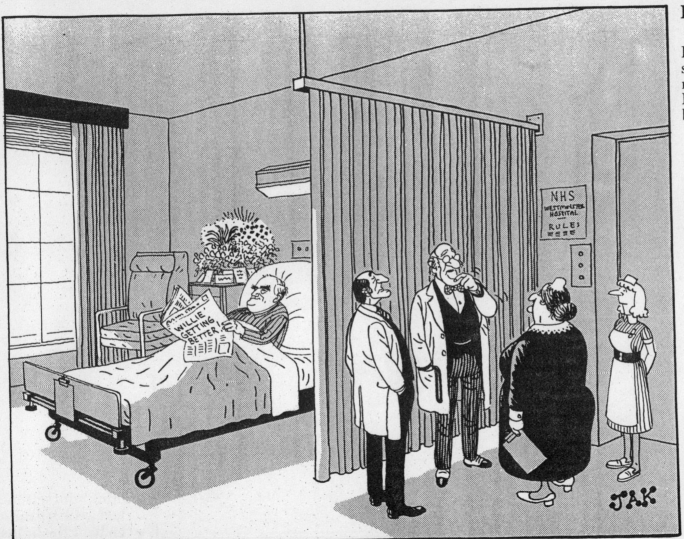

December 17, 1987

Lord Whitelaw had a slight stroke but recovered well (in a National Health Service bed)

"You say he enjoyed his third NHS breakfast running? I think he'd better see a psychiatrist!"

December 18, 1987

The NHS was subject to cutbacks, before the Government announced a cash injection of nearly £100 million for the service.

NHS IMPROVEMENTS

FARRELLS ECONOMIC SKIPS

JAK

"Think yourself lucky ... last week we didn't even have the lights!"

December 23, 1987

Lord King of British
Airways celebrated the
takeover of British
Caledonian.

KING JOHN

December 24, 1987

You've heard of talking turkey, this was a singing one.

"We didn't have the heart to stuff him when he started singing 'I'm dreaming of a White Christmas'!"

December 27, 1987

The season of family goodwill ...

"Never mind sir, next year it'll be your brother-in-law's turn to put up your family at Christmas."

January 4, 1988

Another ex-MI6 man wanted to publish his memoirs but had an injunction slapped on parts of them.

"We find it saves the time of going to the law courts!"

January 13, 1988

At prayers before the new Commons session, an MP interrupted and was banned for a week.

"Order! Order! Silence in the shed or I'll have you all named!"

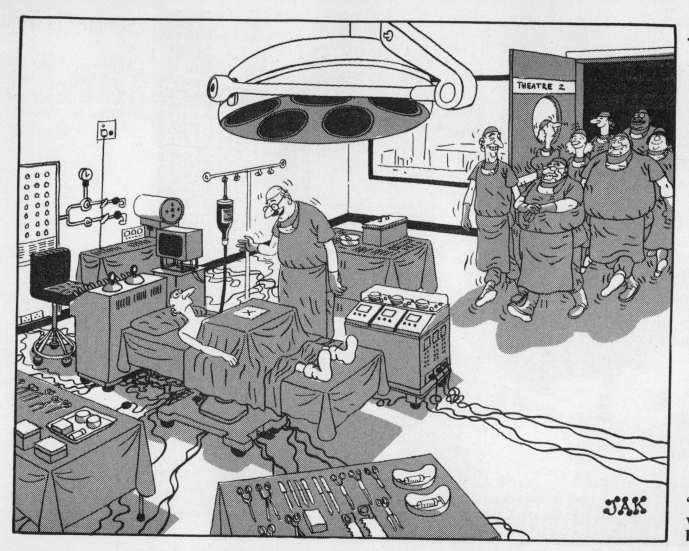

January 14, 1988

Blood transfusion staff in some areas were taking industrial action because their meal allowances were being cut - the allowances were soon restored.

"Do you mind Ribena, we're a bit short of blood?"

January 17, 1988

Liberal leader David Steel was not finding it easy merging with the SDP.

"I think it's David Steel going in for re-indoctrination!"

January 18, 1988

The Liberals and the SDP had another go ...

"Well that's settled, now who's going to present the new merger document to the Press?"

A British woman was given 25 years hard labour in Egypt for smuggling drugs.

"Well do as much as you can!"

Prince Edward took a behind-the-scenes job with Andrew Lloyd Webber's Really Useful Company.

"Can't do anything right! Tell your body-guard to make the tea next time!"

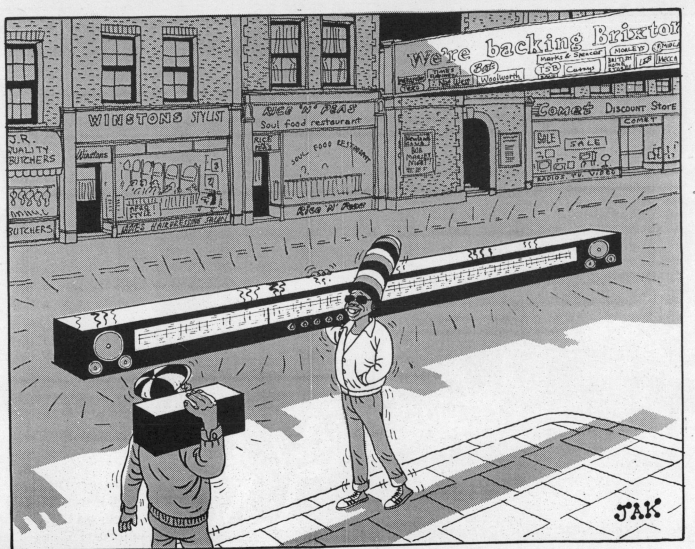

January 21, 1988

Douglas Hurd announced plans for three commercial national radio stations.

"It'll pick up all the new independent radio stations!"

January 25, 1988

The Prince and Princess of Wales were in Australia for bicentenary celebrations.

"Princess Di! Last week it was a flying saucer on the roof of your car!"

January 29, 1988

Westminster City Council were behind a scheme to recruit ex-servicemen and former police personnel for an anti-litter campaign.

"... And the matchstick!"

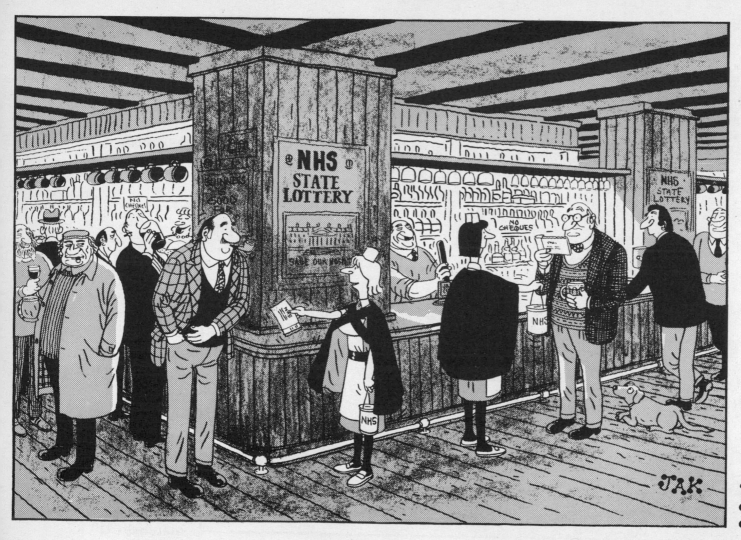

January 31, 1988

A lottery in aid of the NHS seemed like a good idea but eventually was not allowed.

"The first prize is an operation of your choice!"

February 2, 1988

Edwina Currie said people should use money saved for holidays to pay for non-urgent operations.

"Instead of a second holiday, Arthur's had a hair transplant, and I've had a face lift!"

February 3, 1988

Chief Constable James Anderton has become a Roman Catholic.

"Actually, I was going to turn Jewish, but I didn't think I could stand the pain!"

During the House of Lords debate over the controversial Clause 28, intended to stop councils promoting homosexuality, several women abseiled down from the public gallery.

"Sorry, old boy. I should have woken you, but I know how you enjoy your afternoon nap!"

Golf clubs still have the standards ...

"Now Wilkins! The committee can't ban sexy shorts for ladies and allow you to go around exciting them in a string vest, can we?"

February 12, 1988

Dog worshippers gathered at Crufts.

"We didn't even get one placing in the Alsation class!"

February 16, 1988

Britain's Eddie Edwards achieved fame by finishing last in the Winter Olympics ski jumping.

"Well done, Eddie, you've broken the British record!"

February 18, 1988

A Metropolitan Police Chief-inspector was suspended after making allegations about the influence of freemasonry in the Force.

"Sometimes on a cold morning I wish I'd never joined the masons!"

February 24, 1988

Lurid stories emerged about the activities of a TV evangelist in the United States.

February 25, 1988

A certain Press baron became renowned for his litigation ...

"Oh look! There's someone Robert Maxwell isn't suing!"

Church of England
vicars were of course
above suspicion ...

"Rumours that I wa[
perform a 'Jimmy
Swaggart' today are[
totally without
foundation. Mrs
Bagshott and I are
JUST good friends!

March 1, 1988

Estate agents in Chester advertising Welsh property for sale were the victims of fire-bomb attacks by Welsh extremists.

"You set fire to this place once more Taffy and you're sacked!"

March 3, 1988

A British Aerospace-Rover merger was imminent.

"The next one complaining about this altimeter or landing gear gets his joy-stick wrapped around his head!"

March 7, 1988

Police conducted a survey in certain areas and assured motorists that even if found over the limit they would not be prosecuted but given cups of coffee to sober them up - even a lift home if necessary.

"I say! Do you think I could have a large G and T while I wait?"

March 9, 1988

Questions were being asked in the House.

"It must have been Fiona ... I've never seen him that exhausted after a late-night sitting!"

March 10, 1988

A little local difficulty between restaurateur Peter Langan and his partner, Michael Caine.

"Be off with you Caine! You're giving the place a bad name!"

March 14, 1988

Mrs Thatcher and Nigel
Lawson were said to have
fallen out over exchange
rate policy.

"Of course Nigel, if you
don't stop arguing,
there's always the
Ulster job!"

March 16, 1988

A new tunnel is to be dug to link the Docklands Light Railway to Bank and Monument stations.

"Judging by the speed, I think we're on the Northern Line."

March 17, 1988

The Budget put an end t[o]
rich people using forestr[y]
as a tax concession.

"I advised him to burn
down what's left of the
forest for the
insurance money!"

March 22, 1988

The ever-interesting Windsors' saga was in the news again.

"Mon dieu Henri! How many more sons did the Duke of Windsor have on the side?"

March 23, 1988

Lord Wraxall emerged unhurt after being shut i the boot of his car by burglars and driven to nearby woods.

"It's for you, m'lud!"

March 28, 1988

Ian Botham was retracing Hannibal's footsteps in aid of leukaemia research.

"Do stop swearing at the elephants Ian, you'll never make it to the alps at this rate!"

March 29, 1988

Lorries proliferated at Dover thanks to the P and O Ferries strike.

"How long have you been queueing at Dover, mate?"

April 6, 1988

There was talk of
televising court
proceedings.

"Do leave out the
histrionics Mr
Smedley, we're not on
the telly yet!"

April 8, 1988

The actress Maria Aitken, on a drugs charge, was acquitted.

"Are you sure you've retained Sir David Napley if things go wrong?"

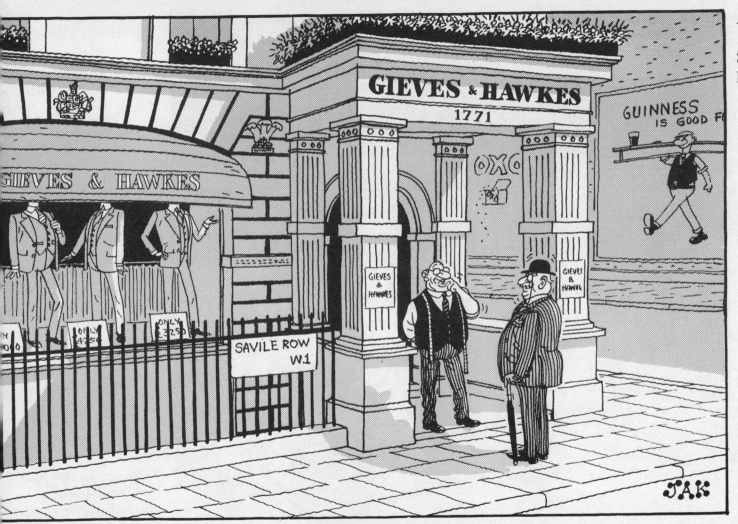

April 10, 1988

Some prominent City
people were in trouble.

"Have you something
with arrows? I've just
been sentenced to five
years in a private
prison!"

April 12, 1988

New DHSS benefits came into effect, not beneficial for everyone.

"The computer will have an answer to your query on the new social security system any minute, sir!"

April 13, 1988

Australian soldiers took over guard duty at Buckingham Palace as part of their country's bicentenary celebrations.

JAK

"Your mascot has just eaten our regimental goat!"

April 15, 1988

As it was taking off, an airliner at Gatwick had swerve off the runway t avoid a plane coming in to land.

"Sorry! We thought it was the emergency runway at Gatwick!"

April 18, 1988

Zola Budd was banned for a year by the international athletics authorities for allegedly taking part in a South African event.

"Bring forth the British Amateur Athletic Association's sacrifice!"

April 26, 1988

Jeffrey Archer bought th
Playhouse Theatre on
London's Embankment

"It's a Jeffrey Archer
season!"

April 28, 1988

Nestle's were making their bid for Rowntrees.

"Ah! Simpson! Are the sherbet dib dabs still British?"

May 4, 1988

Dire threats were made peers who voted for the highly contentious Clause 28.

"As I suspected, it's another gay death threat, m'lud!"

May 6, 1988

Prince Charles objected
to a block of flats which
would overlook
Kensington Palace.

May 10, 1988

Major Ronald Ferguson, the Duchess of York's father, was alleged to have been a regular client at a massage parlour.

"Polo ponies! I thought it was the Household Cavalry on Tuesdays!"

May 12, 1988

Prince Harry had a minor operation.

"We've put Tarquin down for Eton, The Guards, and a hernia operation!"

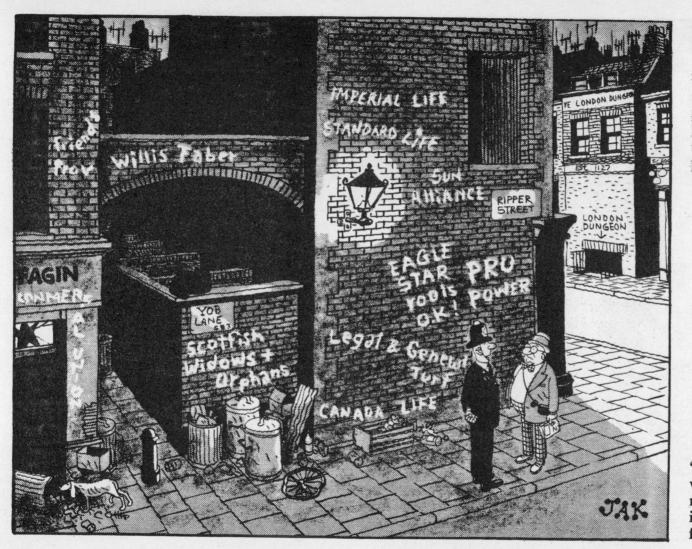

May 13, 1988

An insurance salesman
Yorkshire was beaten u
by four men who didn'
like his sales pitch but
later he talked two of
them into taking out lif
policies ...

"You don't have to
worry about muggers
round here, sir. The
insurance agents have
frightened them off!"

British Satellite Broad-
casting and the BBC
reached an agreement to
broadcast FA Cup and
international matches
exclusively this season.

"So I said, if you're
going watch football
six hours a day, you can
live in there!"

Wimbledon amazed the soccer experts by beating Liverpool in the FA Cup Final.

"Is that the Wigmore Massage Club? Our chairman's put his back out demonstrating the Cup Final penalty save!"

May 18, 1988

A new body headed by Sir William Rees-Mogg is to keep an eye on sex and violence on TV.

"We've taken out the sex and violence - and this is what we've got left for the summer schedules!"

Two cases against alleged
gangs of soccer hooligans
were dropped because the
Judge said police
evidence was
unsatisfactory.

"Never mind precious,
I'm sure they'll get the
paperwork wrong!"

May 24, 1988

The House of Lords, including some Tories, tried to overthrow the Community Charge Bill but were defeated because peers who normally didn't attend were persuaded to turn up and vote for the Government.

"I demand a recount, this one's stuffed!"

May 26, 1988

Soviet military personnel were invited to visit Porton Down as part of the new openness policy.

"Spot! That's a nice name for a mascot!"

June 2, 1988

The Scots Guards complained about a sequence in Tumbledown, a film about the Falklands campaign, and the BBC agreed to a cut.

"... And I got this one for knocking 12 seconds off a BBC film!"

June 3, 1988

The jury in a football hooliganism trial said they felt threatened by the accused's relatives in court.

"Take that expression off your face - I do the jury threatening around here!"

June 7, 1988

Spanish air traffic controllers said their airspace was overcrowded and decided to allow only a certain number of flights to operate.

"British Airwaaaaaayyyyss announce a further deeelaaaayyy in their flights to Sssppppaaaiiiiinnnn!"

Ken Dodd faced tax
evasion charges.

**"Mr Dodd! What
exactly is a tatti-
felarious discum-
knockerating tickling
stick?"**

June 10, 1988

Satellite TV was making its presence felt.

"I suppose it's a fake one, like their burglar alarm!"

June 13, 1988

A report linked
aluminium in water to
Alzheimer's disease
(senile dementia)

"It was all the excuse
Henry needed to avoid
water completely!"

July 3, 1988

The French Archbishop Lefebvre defiantly stood out against the current Roman Catholic leadership and appointed his own bishops.

"I'm afraid I don't know what they're saying, m'dear - it's all Latin to me!"

July 5, 1988

Savoy shareholders voted overwhelmingly against a takeover bid by Trust House Forte.

"Is it safe to eat in the Grill Room yet?"

July 7, 1988

It was decided that SAS witnesses at the inquest into the killing of three IRA members on Gibraltar would be behind a screen but visible to Coroner, counsel and jury.

"Well, good luck in Gibraltar chaps, and remember, short back and sides on your return!"

July 12, 1988

Michael Jackson arrived for a series of concerts.

"Extraordinary uniforms they dress the lift boys in these days!"

July 14, 1988

Black widow spiders were found in grapes imported from the USA.

"Sorry about that sir, there'll be no charge for the grapes!"

August 3, 1988

The Lambeth Conference voted to have women bishops in the Anglican Church.

August 4, 1988

Graham Gooch became England's fourth Test captain in a disastrous cricket season.

"Bird Eye's standing by in case we run out of captains!"

August 18, 1988

Fare increases were planned for long-distanc[e] British Rail commuters.

"We won't be able to afford this luxury when they put the fares up!!"

August 21, 1988

Pubs could stay open all day if they wished.

"I must admit, it doesn't do a great deal for the environment either!"

August 23, 1988

Not everyone wanted to drink all day ...

"Could we just come in for a couple of hours?'

August 24, 1988

Hope springs eternal ...

"I won't make a penny out of this! But all right, mate! Three goldfish and six balloons!"

Postmen went on strike
over a scheme for bonus
payments in London and
the South-East, and
private delivery firms
prepared for a boom.

"Of course he's
smiling, he just tasted
his first private
postman!"